GEARED FOR GROWTH BIBLE STUDIES

GOD CARES

A STUDY IN THE LIFE OF JONAH

BIBLE STUDIES TO IMPACT THE LIVES OF ORDINARY PEOPLE

Written by Nina Drew

The Word Worldwide

CHRISTIAN FOCUS

For details of our titles visit us on our website
www.christianfocus.com

ISBN 1-84550-024-5

10 9 8 7 6 5 4 3 2 1

Published in 2005 by
Christian Focus Publications Ltd, Geanies House,
Fearn, Tain, Ross-shire, IV20 1TW, Scotland
and
WEC International, Bulstrode, Oxford Road,
Gerrards Cross, Bucks, SL9 8SZ

Cover design by Alister MacInnes

Printed and bound by Bell & Bain, Glasgow

CONTENTS

QUESTIONS AND NOTES

ANSWER GUIDE

PREFACE

GEARED FOR GROWTH

**'Where there's LIFE there's GROWTH:
Where there's GROWTH there's LIFE.'**

WHY GROW a study group?

Because as we study the Bible and share together we can

- learn to combat loneliness, depression, staleness, frustration, and other problems
- get to understand and love each other
- become responsive to the Holy Spirit's dealing and obedient to God's Word

and that's GROWTH.

How do you GROW a study group?

- Just start by asking a friend to join you and then aim at expanding your group.
- Study the set portions daily (they are brief and easy: no catches).
- Meet once a week to discuss what you find.
- Befriend others, both Christians and non-Christians, and work away together

see how it GROWS!

WHEN you GROW ...

This will happen at school, at home, at work, at play, in your youth group, your student fellowship, women's meetings, mid-week meetings, churches and communities,

you'll be REACHING THROUGH TEACHING.

INTRODUCTORY STUDY

THE CHARACTERS IN THIS STUDY

There are many inseparable pairs in history and fiction. What do you think of when you hear the name Romeo? Right, Juliet! What about Adam? Yes, Eve. Jack and the Beanstalk (or is it Jack and Jill?) And what about Jonah? I knew you would say the huge fish (perhaps we say whale without thinking). But are Jonah and the fish the main characters in this extraordinary story? Actually the fish is a minor character in this drama. He is only the vehicle God planned to bring His reluctant missionary back to the job to which God had called him.

The main character is GOD, because it all started with God's call to Jonah and without God there would be no book of Jonah. The next character is JONAH who tried unsuccessfully to defy God. Next would be the NINEVITES who turned from their sin at Jonah's preaching. The SAILORS who tried to save Jonah's life are perhaps next in line. And maybe we could give the fish the rank of fifth place.

Is this story fiction or history?

Definitely history! Jonah's name and his father's name are stated. Also his place of residence (2 Kgs. 14:25) and Nineveh, the city to which he was sent. Besides this he is referred to both in Old and New Testaments. Jesus Himself referred to this story and the repentance of the Ninevites. The book bears the stamp of authenticity.

Jonah, the reluctant missionary

Jonah was a reluctant missionary. But was he unique in his reluctance to obey God? Picture Moses standing before the burning bush and hearing God's call to be the deliverer of his nation from slavery in Egypt. 'But God, my nation won't believe me ... I'm not eloquent ... Please send someone else.' Or the young Jeremiah. 'Ah, Lord God, I cannot speak for I am a youth.' And God's reassurance, 'I am giving you the words to speak. I am giving you authority over the nations.'

Both Moses and Jeremiah responded after an initial argument. Or think of Peter who thought himself an utter failure after denying his Lord, yet the call of God came to him to preach Jesus to his nation.

Yet Peter, like Jonah, had one blind spot. He was prejudiced against the Gentile nations and it took a vision from God to get him moving, with some trepidation, towards the house of Cornelius, the Roman centurion, with exciting results. Many of God's people have had reservations when God has called them, and have taken a lot of persuading to obey God's call. Yet God persisted in His call and He still used them greatly.

What of you? What of me?

Are we sometimes reluctant missionaries? How can we know God's will today? How does He call us? He does not usually speak in an audible voice. In fact He usually speaks in such a gentle voice or inner urge that we hardly realise that it is God speaking to us.

Some examples of the way the Lord speaks to us:

GOD'S NUDGE:	Anne has not been to church the past two Sundays. She may be sick. Give her a ring.
REPLY:	I don't know her all that well. Anyway it might not be a convenient time.
GOD'S NUDGE:	Invite your new neighbours in for a cup of coffee.
REPLY:	We don't think they'd be interested. They don't look our type.
GOD'S NUDGE:	You spoke sharply today. You should ring and apologise.
REPLY:	But I was provoked. I'll just act as if all is well, and it'll blow over.
GOD'S NUDGE:	You should pledge a monthly amount for the support of the missionaries.
REPLY:	Plenty of others earn more than I do. I'll just give what I can spare.
GOD'S NUDGE:	Aren't you going to church tonight?
REPLY:	Well there's that good programme on the TV.

FAMILIAR? We all identify with some of these reluctant servants of God, don't we? So often God's callings remain unnoticed, because we don't recognise them as the voice of God. He wants us to have spiritual ears to hear His promptings, which often come in a most unobtrusive way. As the Good Shepherd He cares for us and wants us to follow Him. Like Jonah He may use unusual circumstances to confront us with our disobedience and to get us to turn from our selfish ways.

God will probably not call us to preach in a great city like Nineveh. But He does call us to be His man or His woman in the environment where He has placed us.

There are plenty of spiritually hungry people all around us, people who don't know that God loves and understands them. We, as His missionaries, are called to be lights in the part of the world where we live or work. Perhaps you could share with the group occasions when you have felt God's nudge and ignored it, with later feelings of regret. Or conversely, how you have obeyed one of those gentle nudges, with exciting results.

I suggest that you read this short book of Jonah through several times, to become familiar with the story, before starting on the studies. Then prepare each lesson in advance, writing down your answers to the daily questions, so as to be able to join in with the discussions. The more you put into each study, the more you will receive from it. The studies will be of still greater benefit if you learn the memory verse each week.

Now let's start our study of the book of Jonah.

STUDY 1

RUNNING AWAY

QUESTIONS

DAY 1 *Jonah 1:1-2; 2 Kings 14:23-25.*

a) How is Jonah described?

b) In Jonah 1, what was he charged to do and why?

DAY 2 *Jonah 1:1-2; 3:1-3, 6, 8; 4:11; Genesis 10:11-12.*

a) What do these verses tell us about Nineveh?

b) What problems are associated with large urban areas today? How can Christians help in solving them?

DAY 3 *Jonah 1:3.*

a) How did Jonah respond to God's call?

b) Have you ever wanted to run away from something you knew God had asked you to do? Why?

c) What did Jesus say is the 'secret' of obedience in John 14:23-24?

DAY 4 *Jonah 1:3, 9; 4:1-2.*

a) What did Jonah know about God? Did this knowledge keep him from disobeying?

QUESTIONS (contd.)

b) What warning is given in I Corinthians 10:12, and what advice in James 1:22-25?

DAY 5 *Jonah 1:3; Luke 11:23; 16:13.*

a) Why did Jonah decide to go to Tarshish? What should Jonah have known from Psalm 139:7-12?

b) 'We run away from God when we disobey Him on some issue.' Is this statement true or false? Discuss your answer in the light of the readings from Luke's Gospel.

DAY 6 *Jonah 1:3; Psalm 119:32-40.*

a) How does the psalmist's attitude to God contrast with that of Jonah?

b) What did the psalmist say results from obedience (v. 35)?

c) The psalmist saw prayer as important? What are some of the things he prayed about?

DAY 7 *Jonah 1:3.*

a) What circumstantial evidence probably encouraged Jonah to continue on with his journey to Tarshish once he had arrived in Joppa?

b) What principles of guidance are found in the following verses: Psalm 25:4-5; Proverbs 12:15; John 7:1; Ephesians 5:3-4?

NOTES

Jonah's call

We learn a little more about Jonah from one verse in 2 Kings 14:25. We find that Jonah had already been recognised as a prophet of God: he had given God's message to Jereboam II, around 820 BC. We also learn from this verse that he lived in Gath-Hepher near Nazareth in Galilee. So, as a man of God, to whom God had previously spoken and performed His word, Jonah was recognised as a prophet of God by his nation. He had no difficulty in recognising God's voice, but he didn't like what he heard! The message was short and clear: 'Go to the great city of Nineveh and preach against it, because its wickedness has come up before me.'

Why was Jonah so reluctant to go? Look at a map and gauge the distance between Galilee and Nineveh. Probably about 1000 km through lonely robber-infested desert land. No plane. Not even a bus. Only a little donkey. Not a very inviting prospect. And to whom was he called to go? Not to his own nation, but to mighty Nineveh, capital of Assyria, the greatest empire of antiquity, and the potential enemy of his own little nation.

There were probably other reasons for his disobedience, which we will discuss later. But let us consider whether disobedience to God is ever justified. Isn't that implying, 'I know better than God'? Surely we can trust the God who created us and loves us. Let us be assured that if God commands, He will enable us to carry out what He calls us to do.

God's school of obedience

From the moment we receive Jesus into our lives, we are automatically enrolled in His SCHOOL OF OBEDIENCE. When we consider how much Jesus has done for us in saving us from Satan's kingdom, and bringing us into His kingdom of light and love, we cannot help but recognise that Jesus is our Lord and Master, and find our chief fulfilment in obeying Him. We, like Jonah, are often slow learners. But when we obey, even after a struggle, we find that His will is 'GOOD, PLEASING AND PERFECT' (Rom. 12:2), and later we can rejoice that we have obeyed.

Jonah's defiance

So, instead of travelling northeast Jonah travelled southwest to the port of Joppa (Modern Jaffa) where he found a ship bound for Spain. How providential!
Circumstances seemed to fit perfectly into his plan to get away from God and His unacceptable call on his life. Surely once he reached Spain God wouldn't bother with him. He'd send someone else. But did He? No, God doesn't give up on us so easily.

MEMORY VERSE: 'Trust in the LORD with all your heart and lean not on your own understanding; in all your ways acknowledge him, and he will make your paths straight' (Prov. 3:5, 6).

STUDY 2

FOUND OUT

QUESTIONS

DAY 1 *Jonah 1:1-5.*

a) Describe the storm and its effect on the ship.

b) Think of unexpected 'storms' that may happen to us. What is the difference between those God sends and those sent by the devil (1 Pet. 1:3-7; 5:8.)?

DAY 2 *Jonah 1:4-5, 11.*

a) How did the sailors respond to the storm?

b) Suggest two reasons why the storm did not abate after the sailors had cried out to their own gods? (One reason can be found in Isa. 45:20; 46:5-7.)

DAY 3 *Jonah 1:5-6.*

a) Who found Jonah asleep? What was he asked to do? Why was he to do this?

b) How is the sleeping of Jonah to be deplored and that of Peter in Acts 12:5-6 admired?

DAY 4 *Jonah 1:6.*

a) In what sense is a Christian to remain continually awake (Mark 14:37-38)?

QUESTIONS (contd.)

b) Mark 4:35-41. Discuss the difference between having a 'Jonah' or Jesus on board our lives in a storm.

DAY 5 *Jonah 1:7-8.*

a) Why did the sailors begin to closely interrogate Jonah?

b) What did Moses warn about sin in Numbers 32:20-23?

DAY 6 *Jonah 1:8-10.*

a) What did Jonah say, and what had he to admit? (Do Christians sometimes contradict their testimony by how they live?)

b) To whom do Christians belong (1 Pet. 2:9-12)?

DAY 7 *Jonah 1:9-10; 1 Peter 4:16-18.*

a) Why did the sailors become terrified?

b) In the light of 1 Peter 4:17-18, why is Jonah's storm at sea a warning for all non-Christians?

NOTES

The voyage

Everything seemed favourable: a ship sailing to the furthermost port of the Mediterranean, a lovely blue sky above and calm sea below. What could be more delightful than a Mediterranean cruise lasting several weeks? After a night or two of conflict and a long trek from Galilee to Joppa, Jonah must have felt weary and he was ready to sleep it off to the gentle movement of the ship. He was on his way to Spain. But was he? God had other plans for Jonah.

The storm

'Then the LORD sent a great wind ... and ... a violent storm arose.' How Jonah slept through that storm we cannot imagine. No one else on the ship was sleeping. Everyone was in a panic. Picture the scene as passengers and crew were tossed around in the lurching ship. Then amid the howling of the wind there was the shouting of orders to throw the cargo overboard. There was bedlam as all were yelling out to their gods to save them.

The sleeper

And imagine their amazement and their anger as they came across Jonah, not helping with the handling of the ship or even calling on his God – instead he was sleeping! Hear the captain's exhortation to get up and call on his god. But would that help? Jonah knew it wouldn't. How useless it is to ask God to help us while we are deliberately defying Him. What a disgrace it was that Jonah, God's reluctant missionary, was the only one on board who refused to pray.

The lots

The sailors recognised that this was no ordinary storm. Never had they seen a storm of such intensity. Could it be that they were harbouring a criminal? Perhaps a murderer was on the passenger list, trying to escape justice. They must find out on whose account this storm was upon them. As was common practice in those days, they decided to cast lots. We don't know how this was done. Perhaps the names of all on board were thrown into a receptacle and one name withdrawn. However it was accomplished, Jonah was proved to be the culprit. It was God who had brought about the storm and it was God who identified the cause of it.

Jonah's confession

A rapid questionnaire followed: Are you the culprit? Your occupation? Your present abode? Your country? Your nationality? And his reply: 'I am a Hebrew, and I worship the LORD, the God of heaven, who made the sea and the land'. He also told them he was fleeing from the presence of this great God. His reply put the sailors in a still greater panic. THEIR gods were powerless idols, but Jonah had declared that HIS God was the one who had created all things, including this turbulent sea. Then there was no hope of their survival, since Jonah was running away from this mighty God.

When we disobey God, our sin does not only affect ourselves, but others as well.

Think of the anxiety of the sailors and passengers, of the loss of precious cargo and the possible loss of the ship and many innocent lives. Likewise, our sin can affect our families, friends and, worst of all, the honour of God's name.

MEMORY VERSE: 'O LORD, you have searched me and you know me. You know when I sit and when I rise; you perceive my thoughts from afar' (Ps. 139:1, 2).

STUDY 3

OVERBOARD

QUESTIONS

DAY 1 *Jonah 1:11-12; Acts 16:25-32.*

a) Why did the sailors now feel compelled to do something to Jonah?

b) What caused the jailer to seek out Paul and Silas, and what was he told to do?

DAY 2 *Jonah 1:12.*

a) What solution did Jonah propose and what did he admit?

b) What consequences of Adam and Eve's sin are highlighted in Romans 5:12, 18?

DAY 3 *Jonah 1:12.*

a) What are Christians warned against in Romans 14:13 and 2 Corinthians 6:3?

b) Psalm 51:1-4; 1 Samuel 22:20-23. How can these verses guide us if we feel that we have caused someone hurt or harm?

DAY 4 *Jonah 1:12; Isaiah 53:4-9; 1 Peter 3:18.*

a) Jonah offered to be thrown overboard to spare the sailors. What has the Lord Jesus done for us? (The prophecy in Isa. 53 refers to Him.)

QUESTIONS (contd.)

b) From these verses (Day 4) find at least one important difference between the Lord Jesus and Jonah.

DAY 5 *Jonah 1:13.*

a) What did the sailors discover about their best efforts at rowing?

b) What does Ephesians 2:8,9 and Titus 3:5 say about 'works' and salvation?

DAY 6 *Jonah 1:13-14; Romans 2:14-16.*

a) The unbelieving sailors desired to save Jonah, a Jew. Yet Jonah was reluctant to save an unbelieving city. Comment on this.

b) Why were the sailors fearful of taking Jonah's life?

DAY 7 *Jonah 1:15-17.*

a) List the miracles recorded here. Comment on the one in verse 16.

b) Should we wait until science proves it before believing that Jonah was swallowed by a huge fish?

NOTES

Man overboard

By now Jonah realised that the ship was about to sink. He did not want the sailors punished for his sin, so asked to be thrown overboard. What was in Jonah's mind when he found himself being picked up by a couple of hefty sailors and being heaved over the side of the ship? Did he, in that split second, regret his stubbornness? He had been stubborn to the extent of being willing to die rather than obey the Lord. Now, as he hit the waves it was too late to change his mind – or was it? In children's pictures of the scene we often see a whale poised there with mouth open ready to catch Jonah as he hit the waves. But that's not how it happened (read 2:3-6). Jonah really did go down to the bottom. One commentator believes he actually drowned, and God brought him back to life in the fish's belly, which would make the incident a still more realistic picture of Jesus' death and resurrection. That may or may not be the case. But without the appearance of the fish, Jonah's story would have ended right there.

The great fish

No Bible character has been attacked as much as Jonah. And no part of his life so much as his being swallowed by a fish. The word used can refer to any sea monster, so we have no problem there. The creature is considered by many to be a sperm whale, as there are several documented cases of a sperm whale swallowing a man whole. It is explained in some commentaries that the first part of the whale's stomach is called the laryngeal pouch. When the food enters the water is expelled and the fish in it descend to the main stomach. As Jonah may have been too large to go down to the stomach, he would have remained in the pouch which would contain air. One such case was reported in 1927 when a man fell overboard from a whaling vessel near the Falkland Islands and was recovered later alive in the whale's laryngeal pouch.

The miracle is not so much in the fact that Jonah survived the horrible experience, but that God had the fish in the right place at the right time, and directed it to the right destination. God will go to any length to bring His erring children back into the place of obedience and fellowship with Himself. 'For I know the plans I have for you,' declares the LORD, 'plans to prosper you and not to harm you, plans to give you hope and a future' (Jer. 29:11).

We often imagine that our plans for our lives are better than God's. They never are. God had to bring Jonah into that uncomfortable, dark, hot, sticky, stinky, fishy place in order to bring him back into the place of obedience and blessing. God had better things for Jonah than drowning at sea, a rebel and a failure.

MEMORY VERSE: 'Where can I go from your Spirit? Where can I flee from your presence?' (Ps. 139:7). (What about memorising the following three verses also?)

STUDY 4

REPENTANT

QUESTIONS

DAY 1 *Jonah 2:1-6; Psalm 130.*

a) This is part of what is known as Jonah's prayer of thanksgiving. Where was he thankful and why?

b) What words in Psalm 130 would have encouraged Jonah to pray in his distress? (They encourage us too!)

DAY 2 *Jonah 2:3; Genesis 50:15-21.*

a) Why could Jonah say that God had tossed him into the sea?

b) How did Joseph come to view all that had happened to him?

DAY 3 *Jonah 2:4; Luke 15:11-24.*

a) Why might Jonah have thought himself banished or cast out of God's presence?

b) Did he allow these negative thoughts keep him from seeking God again?

c) Did the prodigal son in Luke 15 allow his past to keep him from going back to his father? What happened when he returned?

QUESTIONS (contd.)

DAY 4 *Jonah 2:6; Proverbs 16:25; James 1:14-15.*

a) Trace Jonah's steps downward (1:3, 5). To where has he gone down now?

b) Do you think he thought he would ever have sunk so low when he took his first wrong step? Discuss the dangers of taking the first wrong step.

DAY 5 *Jonah 2:2-7.*

a) When did Jonah remember the Lord?

b) Who prayed at the last moment in Luke 23:40-43? Was his prayer answered?

c) Jonah's prayer rose to God even if he couldn't go the temple. What picture of prayer is given in Revelation 8:3-5?

DAY 6 *Jonah 2:8-9; Ecclesiastes 5:1-7.*

a) What did Jonah promise?

b) What warning is given about vows in Ecclesiastes?

DAY 7 *Psalm 18:4-6; 31:6-22; 42:7; 69:1; 116:17, 18.*

a) Why do you think Jonah was familiar with these Psalms?

b) Discuss briefly how Psalms like these can help us worship God.

NOTES

Jonah's prayer

And now that he has submitted to God, he is able to pray. He didn't have to kneel. He didn't have to open his mouth – that might have been disastrous! He just had to lift his heart to God in submission and trust. We too can pray at any time in any place, and we can know our loving Father will hear and respond. What a contrast to the Jonah of chapter 1! We have no record of Jonah calling on God when exhorted to do so in the ship. Now, inside the fish he willingly calls on Him. He declares, 'You answered me. You heard me'. He had fled from his country to be away from the presence of the Lord. Now he expresses his fear that he is ABOUT TO BE BANISHED from the Lord's presence, that he would never again enjoy the fellowship of God's people in His holy temple.

What brought about his change of attitude? Maybe it was FEAR of death and the judgment. Fear can be a good thing when it drives us to God. Distress can be our ally when it causes us to cry out to Him.

> 'In my distress, O LORD, I called to you.'
> 'When I felt my life slipping away, then, O LORD, I prayed to you' (GNB).

Jonah describes in graphic terms his terrifying experience, as he begins to drown. No doubt it dawned on Jonah as he felt his life slipping away that he had been a failure, that he had let down badly the God who loved him. In his spirit he cried out to God and God had his transport back to Joppa already arranged.

How much of this prayer was prayed while he was drowning, and how much in the fish, it is hard to say. But he had three days – sticky, smelly, stuffy days – to meditate on his ways, and to renew his vows to the Lord. At some stage of his life he had promised to serve the Lord, and had gone back on that vow. Now he renews that vow. His repentance is complete. He ends his prayer with the assertion, 'Salvation comes from the LORD'. We see in Jonah's prayer assurance of God's answer, recognition of God's sovereignty, thanksgiving, and promise of future obedience. What a model for us!

Jonah's deliverance

Only the Lord could have arranged such a novel means of transport and steered the vehicle to the beach from where Jonah had originally started out on his epic voyage. 'Then the Lord ordered the fish to spew Jonah up on the beach, and it did' (GNB). Not only do the wind and waves obey the creator God, but His living creatures are also under His command. Only man has been given the capacity to disobey his creator.

MEMORY VERSE: 'If we confess our sins, he is faithful and just and will forgive us our sins and purify us from all unrighteousness' (1 John 1:9).

STUDY 5

RE-COMMISSIONED

QUESTIONS

DAY 1 *Jonah 2:10; Hebrews 12:4-11.*

a) Hebrews 12:4-11 states that discipline though painful has a purpose. How had this been true of Jonah inside the fish?

b) How might Jonah have felt as he stood on dry ground?

DAY 2 *Jonah 2:10-3:2.*

a) What happened a second time?

b) 1 Corinthians 5:1-5; 2 Corinthians 2:5-11. How does Paul deal here with failure in the life of a Christian?

DAY 3 *Jonah 3:1-2.*

a) John 21:15-19; Acts 15:36-39; 2 Timothy 4:11. Was Jonah unique in being re-commissioned after failure? What happened to both Peter and Mark?

b) Even if God has forgiven us we may find it hard to forgive ourselves. How can we overcome this?

DAY 4 *Jonah 3:1-2; Romans 6:1-15.*

Some people might say that it doesn't matter if we sin because God will always forgive us. How does Paul refute this suggestion in Romans 6:1-15?

QUESTIONS (contd.)

DAY 5 *Jonah 3:1-2; 2 Timothy 3:15-17.*

a) Why is reading the Bible important in finding out what God wants us to do?

b) Have you a verse of Scripture that God has used to bless and guide you?

DAY 6 *Jonah 1:2; 3:1-2;*

a) What message was Jonah to proclaim?

b) I Corinthians 15:1-7. What important message have we to pass on to others?

DAY 7 *Jonah 3:3.*

a) What was Jonah careful to do now? What kind of obedience is illustrated in Joshua 11:15; John 8:28; 12:49?

b) What are we reminded about Nineveh?

NOTES

The re-commissioning

It is most likely that the fish 'spewed up' Jonah on the shore near to Joppa from where he had originally sailed. (God often brings us back to the point of failure before He re-commissions us.) Jonah faced his failure and repented.

So let's think about what repentance means. It isn't only being sorry that I have done wrong, or that my wrong has been found out. It is something much deeper. It means RIGHT ABOUT TURN. Instead of going west to Spain, Jonah was to go northeast to Nineveh. Repentance implies ongoing obedience. It means that, instead of ruling my own life, I surrender the running of my life to God.

Jonah understood that. He recognised the seriousness of his sin in defying God and his foolishness in imagining that he could run away from God's presence. He was now thankful that that had been impossible. And maybe as he pondered these things he realised that God really loved him, that He would go to any length to bring him back to Himself.

Having repented, God's word came to him again: 'Go to the great city of Nineveh and proclaim to it the message I give you'. God's re-commissioning Jonah was evidence that He still cared for and regarded him as His trusted servant. Isn't it great that God doesn't give up on us when we have failed. No argument now. 'Jonah obeyed the word of the LORD and went to Nineveh.'

His destination

Let's take a look at Nineveh. It was the capital of the great Assyrian empire.

According to Genesis 10:8-12, it was founded by Nimrod who ruled over a vast kingdom away back three generations after Noah. But we don't hear much more of Nineveh again until God's call came to Jonah in the eighth century BC. By then the city was immense, and surrounded by walls so huge that six chariots could ride abreast on top of them. It contained great palaces and immense sculptures which have been excavated in recent years. As well as calling it 'a very important city', God described it in His first call to Jonah as a wicked city. It seems that every form of wickedness was practised within its walls.

God did not immediately give Jonah the message he was to proclaim. But somewhere on the long journey He must have made it clear to him. What a lesson for us! So often we try to witness for Jesus out of our human knowledge, and wonder why it is fruitless. God wants us to look to Him to show us how to witness effectively. Jesus is our supreme example in this. Though He was the eternal Son of God, He said, 'I do nothing on my own but speak just what the Father has taught me' (John 8:28 and 12:49).

We have the Holy Spirit within us who will guide us in all our conversations, if we will only look in faith to Him.

MEMORY VERSE: '"You are my witnesses", declares the LORD, "and my servant whom I have chosen"' (Isa. 43:10).

STUDY 6

PREACHING

QUESTIONS

DAY 1 *Jonah 3:3-4; 1 Corinthians 2:1-5..*

a) What message did Jonah have to proclaim?

b) In what way could Jonah have been like Paul (1 Cor. 2:1-5)? What did Paul preach that Jonah could not?

DAY 2 *Jonah 3:5.*

a) What was the initial reaction of the Ninevites to Jonah's preaching?

b) Psalm 10:11-14. What reason is given for the wicked not obeying God in this Psalm? Were the Ninevites like this?

c) 1 Thessalonians 2:13. How did the Thessalonians receive Paul's message?

DAY 3 *Jonah 3:5-9.*

a) What indications are there that the people were earnest in seeking God?

b) How did the king react to the news of Jonah's preaching?

QUESTIONS (contd.)

DAY 4 *Jonah 3:6-9; Jeremiah 36:1-3, 16, 20-26.*

a) Contrast the reaction of King Jehoiakim and the king of Nineveh to God's message. (How are we responding to God's Word?)

b) Discuss the pros and cons of the king of Nineveh issuing this decree.

DAY 5 *Jonah 3:8; Isaiah 55:6-7.*

a) What advice of the king is repeated in Isaiah 55:6-7?

b) What was the king unsure about? How would the verses just read in Isaiah have reassured him?

c) What is emphasised in I John 1:9.

DAY 6 *Jonah 3:10; James 2:20-26.*

a) To what is attributed God's change of attitude towards Nineveh?

b) What does James say is the connection between what we do (works) and faith?

DAY 7 *Matthew 12:38-41.*

a) What aspects of Jonah's story does Jesus refer to?

b) Compare and contrast the people of Jesus' day with those in Nineveh.

NOTES

Jonah's preaching

Picture the scene with me as one weary plainly dressed little foreigner enters the massive gates of the great city and walks along its paved streets gazing at all the luxury and finery on every hand. Would anyone believe his message? He continues all day to the stares of the passers-by. Now he knows his time has come. The message of God is burning hot in his breast. He stops, and begins to proclaim in a loud voice, 'In forty days Nineveh will be destroyed!' The crowd gathers, people stare. Who is this stranger who speaks with such a note of authority? People begin to think about their evil lives. They look around on the greatest city on earth. Could the great God of this stranger destroy their massive city? Conviction begins to grip their hearts. The crowds increase. Then someone notifies the king. Did Jonah relate to the king his attempt to escape from God and his amazing passage back to his land? Possibly. Scripture is sometimes tantalisingly brief, details are not always given.

Nineveh's repentance

Many people have already put off their gorgeous silk garments and clothed themselves with sackcloth, an international sign it seems of repentance. It is stated not that the people believed Jonah, but God. They recognised the authority of God through the words of His servant.

Then the king gives the order, 'Do not let man or beast, herd or flock, taste anything; do not let them eat or drink. But let man and beast be covered with sackcloth. Let everyone call urgently on God. Let them give up their evil ways and their violence.'

And the people obey, not because they were afraid of the king, but because they are afraid of God. Even the animals are to be involved in the national repentance.

God's changed attitude

God saw, not only the sackcloth and the fasting, but the hearts of the people. He saw them turn away from their evil ways. So the Lord 'repented' (AV), which means that He changed His mind and His attitude towards them, because they had changed their attitude towards Him.

Why did Nineveh repent?

Why did a great nation turn to God on the preaching of one unknown stranger?
Was it because:

1. Jonah had OBEYED God even though it was costly?
2. The Holy Spirit was free to work mightily through His obedient servant?
3. God knew the time was ripe. It was either repentance or destruction. Their sin had

reached epidemic proportions. Through the Holy Spirit's work in their lives, they too saw the alternatives and turned in repentance to God.

4. As God had already planned that the Redeemer would come and take the punishment for these people, He was able to justly forgive them.

God does everything He can to bring people to repentance, so that He will not have to destroy. His desire is to forgive.

MEMORY VERSE: 'If my people who are called by my name, will humble themselves and pray and seek my face and turn from their wicked ways, then will I hear from heaven and will forgive their sin and will heal their land' (2 Chron. 7:14).

STUDY 7

RESENTFUL

QUESTIONS

DAY 1 *Jonah 3:4,10-4:1; Matthew 7:1-5.*

a) How might the Ninevites have felt on Day 40, and then on Day 41?

b) How did Jonah feel on Day 41?

c) Before we condemn Jonah, what did Jesus say we should be doing (Matt. 7:1-5)?

DAY 2 *Jonah 4:1-2.*

a) What apparently did Jonah not want to see happen?

b) What had made him suspect that God would withdraw his threat to Nineveh?

DAY 3 *Jonah 4:1-2.*

a) How can verses like Isaiah 55:7-9 help us accept the way God sometimes acts towards us and others?

b) Ephesians 4:31-5:2; Colossians 3:12-13. On what is a Christian to mould his or her behaviour towards others?

QUESTIONS (contd.)

DAY 4 *Jonah 4:1-2; Psalm 42:9-11.*

a) How did Jonah express his feelings? What can we commend and what should we criticise in this prayer of his?

b) When is it right for us to pray out of a sense of anger?

DAY 5 *Jonah 4:1-3.*

Look at the five reasons suggested in the Notes (p. 29) for Jonah's anger.

a) Which one(s) do you think might help explain his attitude?

b) Why are none of these suggested reasons valid?

DAY 6 We may think Jonah's attitude to Nineveh strange. Are we any better? Have we our own 'reasons' for not sharing the gospel with others of a different race or culture? Look up Acts 1:8; John 14:6. Which misconception listed below does each of these verses answer?

a) 'All religions lead to God. Isn't it arrogant to think that our religion is better than other people's?'

b) 'The need is so great at home so why should we send people abroad?'

DAY 7 *Jonah 4:3; Philippians 1:20-26.*

a) Why might Jonah have wanted to die? (As an angry man was he in a position to make a good decision?)

b) Why did Paul say death was better? Why was Paul prepared and glad to go on living?

NOTES

Reasons for Jonah's resentment

We would be happier if the story of Jonah had ended with chapter 3, but God always 'tells it as it is'. Now a side of Jonah's character is portrayed that we would prefer not to see. If we go back to the end of chapter 3 we see that God has changed His mind and His attitude towards the Ninevites, because they had changed their attitude towards God. And now Jonah is angry and resentful.

Let's look at the incident from Jonah's point of view. God had given him a message to proclaim: 'Forty more days and Nineveh will be overturned'. He had proclaimed it, resulting in a revival that would have made headlines today. But here lay the confusion. God had said nothing about His willingness to forgive them if they repented. Jonah, however, knew God's character, since God had revealed it long ago to Moses (Exod. 34:6). So he had a suspicion that God would be merciful, and he didn't like that thought one little bit. He had hoped they wouldn't repent and was angry and resentful when they did.

What was the reason for his anger and confusion? Various reasons have been put forward:

1. Jonah believed his nation to be God's special nation, and regarded all others as inferior.
2. Jonah considered Nineveh to be such an evil city, that it didn't deserve God's mercy.
3. He knew that the great nation of Assyria – of which Nineveh was capital – was a potential threat to little Israel.
4. He realised that if God didn't destroy Nineveh, his reputation as a prophet would suffer.
5. He didn't trust the repentance of the Ninevites. He was sure that as soon as the danger period was past, they would return to their evil ways and God's holy name would be a laughing stock among them. He cared for God's reputation as he did for his own.

He was very resentful. Why had God gone back on His word? So he challenged God on the subject. Our God doesn't mind if we bring our confusions and hurts to Him. He wants us to be honest with Him, so that He can help us understand His ways. God cares for us.

Our resentments

Are we ever confused at God's dealings with us? We have prayed earnestly for the healing of some loved one and that person has died. We felt God leading us in a certain direction, but it did not work out. We have wanted to take up some Christian ministry, but have found ourselves caring for an elderly parent. So many things can bring confusion. We can very easily grow upset and resentful at God's dealings with us.

The answer is simply TRUST GOD. Isaiah 55:8, 9 says: 'For my thoughts are not your thoughts, neither are your ways my ways, declares the LORD. As the heavens are higher than the earth, so are my ways higher than your ways and my thoughts than your thoughts'.

God is working out for us something infinitely better than we could work out for ourselves. Remember that He is GOD – all-knowing, all-wise, always present, all-powerful, always caring and, above all, all-compassionate.

MEMORY VERSE: Isaiah 55:8, 9 quoted in the last paragraph.

STUDY 8

GOD'S REPROVED SERVANT

QUESTIONS

DAY 1 *Jonah 4:4.*

a) How did God respond to Jonah's anger? (We find the same approach later in v. 9.) Was He condoning or condemning Jonah's behaviour?

b) What is said about anger in James 1:19-21?

DAY 2 *Jonah 4:5-6.*

a) Why did Jonah go outside the city?

b) What problems did Jonah face outside the city? Could he blame God for them or were they self-inflicted?

DAY 3 *Jonah 4:6.*

a) How did God show His care for Jonah again? What is emphasised about this provision in verse 10?

b) Was Jonah right to be glad about what God had done?

c) Think of something you are glad that God has recently given you.

DAY 4 *Jonah 4:7-10.*

a) What plunged Jonah into despair again? (Can you imagine his frantic efforts to save the vine!)

QUESTIONS (contd.)

b) Go back to your answer to Day 3(c). Is it possible for us to get so caught up in our own little world that we forget the needs of others?

c) What lesson does God teach Jonah from this incident concerning the vine?

DAY 5 *Jonah 4:10-11; John 3:16-17; Romans 5:11.*

a) Summarise again the lesson that God was trying to teach Jonah? Do you think Jonah learned it?

b) God was concerned for Nineveh. How did He later *prove* His concern not just for Nineveh but for the world?

DAY 6 *Psalm 22:27; 86:9; Isaiah 45:22-23.*

How do these verses reinforce the book of Jonah's message that even in the Old Testament period, God was concerned for the nations of the world?

DAY 7 *2 Timothy 3:14-17; 2 Peter 1:20-21.*

a) As it is part of Scripture, what should reading and studying the book of Jonah do for us?

b) What have you found most helpful or challenging as you have read and studied this book?

NOTES

Jonah's depression

In reply to Jonah's prayer that he might die God asks him a question: 'Is it right for you to be angry?' And the rest of the chapter is God's explanation as to why it is NOT right for Jonah to be angry.

Jonah's work was completed. He should have returned home, but he still wanted to linger. He found some leafy branches and made a shelter for himself overlooking the city so that he might see what would become of it. Did he still hope that God would destroy it? Did he hope that now the danger period was over the people would return to their evil ways and God would change His attitude and be obliged to destroy the city? Whatever the reason, he continued to sit under his flimsy shelter – sulking! It has been said that Jonah sat waiting for God to come round to his way of thinking, but God in fact, was waiting for Jonah to come round to His way of loving!

The object lesson

God then gave Jonah an object lesson to reassure him. This part of the story is not so easy to understand. He caused a leafy plant to grow up and give additional shelter to His weary disillusioned servant and Jonah was grateful. Then the next day He caused a worm to destroy the plant. And Jonah was not amused! Again Jonah's self-pity came to the fore: 'It is better for me to die than to live'. Not long before this Jonah had asked the sailors to throw him into the raging torrent, but then, as the terrors of death faced him, he had cried out to the Lord (ch. :2) and God had saved him. What changeable moods we all can have at times!

Again God repeated the question 'Is it right for you to be angry – about the plant?'

God used this acted parable as an illustration to reprove His servant and show him the value of the many thousands of people in Nineveh. Jonah had been inconvenienced by the removal of the plant that he had not put there in the first place. Yet he could feel no pity for the many thousands of Ninevites who could have been facing destruction.

Jonah had expected God to be merciful to him by protecting him from the heat of the sun. Yet he did not expect Him to be merciful to a city of over a million inhabitants, including 120,000 young children. If the angels rejoice over one sinner who repents, how much rejoicing must there have been over a whole city turning to God. We hope Jonah learned the lesson. We hope that he was reassured that God was still in total control.

The story's end

The story ends there. And what became of Nineveh? Sure enough they later returned to their evil ways, enslaving country after country, including the ten northern tribes of Israel. God had patience with Nineveh for another 150 years. But then it was totally destroyed by the

Babylonians. God loves to show mercy, but when His oft repeated warnings are not heeded, God must resort to judgment. (See Nahum and Zechariah for the later destruction of Nineveh).

MEMORY VERSE: 'Search me, O God, and know my heart; test me and know my anxious thoughts. See if there is any offensive way in me, and lead me in the way everlasting' (Ps. 139:23, 24).

ANSWER GUIDE

The following pages contain an Answer Guide. It is recommended that answers to the questions be attempted before turning to this guide. It is only a guide and the answers given should not be treated as exhaustive.

GUIDE TO STUDY 1

DAY 1 a) As God's servant and prophet (he had already spoken on God's behalf); the son of Amittai from Gath Hepher.
b) To go to Nineveh and preach against it because of its wickedness.

DAY 2 a) Great, important, wicked, a place of violence, populous. Founded by Nimrod. A capital city as it had a king.
b) Suggestions: unemployment, drug addiction, poor housing, crime, etc. Suggestions: prayer, support for Christian ministries in inner city areas, voting for good local authority policies, etc.

DAY 3 a) He ran away from the Lord.
b) Personal.
c) Love.

DAY 4 a) He acknowledged God as Creator, as One who was gracious, compassionate, slow to anger and full of love.
No.
b) No one reaches a stage in this life where it is impossible not to sin. We have to be continually on our guard against failure. James says that truth is to be obeyed; it is not enough to know or be aware of facts about God. Our lives are to be transformed to be like Christ.

DAY 5 a) To flee from the Lord. God is everywhere present.
b) The answer must be, "Yes". Jesus indicates that there is no neutrality in the Christian life: we are either for or against the Lord Jesus.

DAY 6 a) The psalmist was eager to obey. He was wanting to 'run' (v. 32 NIV) in the path of God's commands. Jonah disobeyed and ran away.
b) Delight and satisfaction.
c) Prayer was important at every stage: he prayed for understanding and direction; he prayed for a willingness to turn away from things that would prevent him from obeying (vv. 36, 37).

DAY 7 a) He found a ship going in this direction and he was able to pay the fare.
b) Prayer and a willingness to be led by God (Ps. 25:4); helpful advice from Christian friends and leaders (Prov. 12:15); circumstances (Jesus avoided the Jews, John 7:1); not going against anything specifically revealed to be contrary to God's Word (Eph. 5:3-4).

GUIDE TO STUDY 2

DAY 1 a) It was violent and threatened the ship; it had come about as a result of a great wind sent by God.
b) Illness, disappointments, etc. God seeks to mature and disciple us; He has our good in mind. The devil seeks our destruction.

DAY 2 a) They were terrified, started to pray and threw the cargo overboard.
b) They were crying out to mere gods who could not even hear, never mind answer. A calm sea would have encouraged the sailors to continue on with their journey and God wanted Jonah in Nineveh. Sometimes unanswered prayer is for our good.

DAY 3 a) The captain. To pray to his 'god' for help. The captain knew that everything humanly possible had been done to save the ship but without success.
b) Jonah was careless about the plight of the sailors. He could have been helping and, more important, praying.
Peter was unafraid of death as his life was in God's hands.

DAY 4 a) A Christian is to remain alert spiritually to avoid temptation. He is to be ready for the sudden return of the Lord Jesus.
b) With Jesus we can make it through any storm. With a Jonah we can lose almost everything.

DAY 5 a) God had overruled the casting of lots to make it fall on Jonah.
b) Though we try, we cannot keep our sin hidden from God.

DAY 6 a) That he was a Hebrew and a worshipper of the LORD, the God of heaven and Creator of everything. He had to admit that he was running away from God.
b) They belong to God; they are His people.

DAY 7 a) They appeared more disturbed than Jonah about the consequence of disobedience. They were thinking perhaps that they did not know how to 'appease' this God who must be great to have sent this storm.
b) If God takes time to chastise the Christian (which at times may appear severe), then those who have never repented can expect a greater judgment.

GUIDE TO STUDY 3

DAY 1

a) The sea was getting even more violent.
b) The earthquake and events surrounding it (the singing of Paul and Silas, the prisoners not escaping, etc.). He wanted to know what he had to do to be saved.

DAY 2

a) He offered to be thrown overboard; he admitted he was the cause of the storm.
b) Sin has entered the world bringing death and condemnation to all. All are sinners.

DAY 3

a) Of doing something that would cause others to stumble or fall into sin.
b) Seek forgiveness from God. Practical support: David promised to look after Abiathar who had lost all his family.

DAY 4

a) He died in our place and for our sins; He bore the punishment for them; we can obtain forgiveness, peace and healing.
b) He was sinless while Jonah was living in disobedience and was the cause of the storm.

DAY 5

a) They achieved nothing; it was impossible to reach land.
b) Salvation comes by grace through faith in the Lord Jesus; we cannot save ourselves.

DAY 6

a) Personal. With what little knowledge they had, the sailors gave greater respect to Jonah's God than Jonah himself.
b) They knew in their hearts they would be accountable for the death of an innocent man.

DAY 7

a) At least three: the calming of the sea, the conversion of the sailors and the provision of the fish for Jonah.
God overruled the disobedience of Jonah for the conversion of the sailors.
b) No. The Bible is God's Word and can be trusted.

GUIDE TO STUDY 4

DAY 1

a) He was still in the fish! Jonah 2:2 probably refers to an earlier prayer of Jonah (whether inside or outside the fish is not clear). He knew that God had answered this cry for help and even though his troubles were not over he could start rejoicing.
b) That though God is holy He is also a God who loves and forgives.

DAY 2

a) He recognised that God had taken the initiative in dealing with him. God had not only allowed but had also constrained the sailors to do this.
b) As God's way of sparing the nation of Israel.

DAY 3

a) He had failed to go to Nineveh and had deliberately tried to run away from God.
b) No. The devil will do everything to keep us from seeking God including reminding us how big a failure we have been, etc. Failure need never be final.
c) No. He found the father running to him; he was treated as a son.

DAY 4

a) He had gone down to Joppa, down into the ship and then down to sleep. He had reached the bottom of the sea (the 'roots of the mountains').
b) Discussion. James 1:14, 15 pictures the fateful consequences when we move from temptation to desire, sinning and then death.

DAY 5

a) At the last moment as his life was ebbing away.
b) One of the criminals crucified with Jesus. Yes!
c) Prayer is pictured as rising up before God. Even if we feel shut in God can still hear our prayers.

DAY 6

a) He promised to sacrifice (resume his worship of God) and pay his vows (probably to do whatever God asked of him again).
b) We are to be serious in making and then in fulfilling any vows we make (marriage vows, for example).

DAY 7

a) He had adopted their language as part of his prayer.
b) They encourage us to bring every aspect of our lives before God. As with Jonah, they supply us with words with which to address God. They teach us to believe in God's ultimate goodness no matter how things appear on the surface, etc.

GUIDE TO STUDY 5

DAY 1 a) Physically he had to endure the pain of surviving inside the fish (some suggest his skin would have been bleached as a result). Emotionally he would not have known when his ordeal would be over, etc. He had started to pray again and was in touch with God again.
b) Relieved, feeling rather groggy and smelly but anxious to obey, etc.

DAY 2 a) God's word came to him again telling him to go to Nineveh.
b) He insisted on discipline (exclusion from the church). Love and forgiveness was then to be extended to the person disciplined.

DAY 3 a) No. Both were not excluded from future Christian service because of past failure.
b) We need to really believe that God has forgiven us and act upon it.

DAY 4 He argues that it is inconceivable to think like this. Becoming a Christian (symbolised in baptism) means dying to sin in order to live a new life before God.

DAY 5 a) God speaks by the Holy Spirit through His Word. (See also answer to Study 1, Day 7(b).)
b) Personal.

DAY 6 a) The Lord's message, the message that God would give him. Perhaps the details of what he had to say were only given later.
b) The gospel message with its emphasis upon the death and resurrection of Jesus Christ.

DAY 7 a) To obey and go to Nineveh. An example of total obedience.
b) It was a very important city. (Commentators are divided as to whether three days was the time to walk around the city or through it.).

GUIDE TO STUDY 6

DAY 1 a) That in forty more days Nineveh would be overthrown.
b) Like Paul he may not have felt eloquent for the task. He may also have trembled as he preached, feeling weak and fearful. (God looks for obedience and not ability.)
Jonah could not preach about Jesus Christ and His crucifixion.

DAY 2 a) They believed God; they believed they would be judged unless they repented.
b) They didn't take God seriously; they didn't believe He would call them to account – but He would. No.
c) They received it as coming from God and believed it.

DAY 3 a) They proclaimed a fast and put on sackcloth as a sign of mourning.
b) He got off his throne, wore clothes of mourning, sat in the dust and made a proclamation.

DAY 4 a) Jehoiakim was unmoved (v. 24) and unwilling to repent. He deliberately burned the message and would have killed Jeremiah. The king of Nineveh's repentance is covered in Day 3.
b) Any discussion should note the good example set by the king. A country will prosper from good legislation. A decree, however, may lead people to do things because they fear a king rather than God; obedience can become external and worthless.

DAY 5 a) To seek and call on God; the wicked are to give up their evil ways.
b) The king was unsure of God's attitude to their repentance or whether they would be forgiven. God's mercy and desire to pardon is emphasised in Isaiah.
c) Forgiveness and cleansing is possible when we confess our sins.

DAY 6 a) His compassion and the Ninevites' changed behaviour.
b) Faith will be evidenced by what we do? God saw that what the Ninevites did was an expression of their inner mourning over sin and not simply as something to do in order to obtain His favour.

DAY 7 a) The length of Jonah's stay inside the fish (three days and three nights); the preaching of Jonah and the repentance of the men of Nineveh.
b) They both were wicked but only those in Nineveh repented.

GUIDE TO STUDY 7

DAY 1

a) Day 40 – anxious, concerned, wondering if their repentance had been accepted by God. Day 41 – relieved, glad that their city had been spared.
b) Jonah was upset and angry.
c) We should be examining our own lives in order to ensure we have no hypocritical attitudes towards others.

DAY 2

a) The city of Nineveh spared.
b) The nature of God, that He was gracious, compassionate, slow to anger and full of love; One who didn't delight in sending calamity.

DAY 3

a) God works according to His Divine mind and not our human one. We need to see things from God's perspective.
b) On their experience of God's forgiveness towards them in Christ and on the self-sacrificial love of the Lord Jesus.

DAY 4

a) In prayer to God.
Commend: It is always good to pour out our feelings to God.
Verbalising our frustrations often leads to new perspectives. Praying is better than retaliating ourselves.
Criticism: There appears to be no intention to learn from God (Ps. 139:23-24). Unlike Job, Jonah is not prepared to bow and worship when everything goes wrong (Job 1:20-22). It is full of the personal pronoun 'I'.
b) When we are deeply concerned about the injustice, corruption, greed, etc. that exists around us.

DAY 5

a) Personal
b) Some suggestions might include: The Jews failed to see their role as a blessing to the world. No one deserves God's mercy, not even the Jews. Israel's future depended on its obedience to God and not on the threat from its neighbours. Jonah was being selfish thinking of his own reputation. We must leave the outcome of our obedience to God with Him.

DAY 6

a) John 14:6 – Jesus is the unique way to God. Unless they hear about Him they will never get to heaven.
b) Acts 1:8. God expects us to witness to all.

DAY 7

a) Perhaps he was feeling frustrated and humiliated as he perceived his reputation as a prophet gone, etc. (No.).
b) He would be with Christ. He was prepared to go on living to help the believers; he was more concerned about others than himself.

GUIDE TO STUDY 8

DAY 1 a) He asked a question. God was neither condoning nor condemning. He was still being very patient with Jonah. (He had shown compassion to Nineveh.)
b) Sinful anger does no good for us spiritually. Our lives are to be governed instead by God's Word.

DAY 2 a) He was still hoping perhaps that God would destroy the city.
b) Loneliness and all the discomfort of living in this flimsy shelter. No doubt 'Yes'. He could perhaps have gone home or been welcome in the city. Anger, resentment, etc., always hurt the one who harbours them.

DAY 3 a) He made a vine or gourd grow up to provide protection. Jonah had nothing to do with it being there.
b) Undoubtedly yes.
c) Personal. Suggestions could be health, job, family, etc.

DAY 4 a) The loss of the vine and his subsequent exposure to the sun and wind.
b) Undoubtedly 'Yes'. We can become too self-centred.
c) As Jonah had become fond of and attached to a simple plant he hadn't produced or tended so how much more then is God right to be concerned about the people of Nineveh.

DAY 5 a) God is concerned for the nations of the world. Though the story ends abruptly its preservation is perhaps an indication that Jonah did repent of his unreasonable attitude.
b) The death of the Lord Jesus on the cross.

DAY 6 God is described as being worshipped by all the nations. Mission has always been central to the heart of God. God fully disclosed His purpose when Jesus Christ came into the world (Gal. 4:4).

DAY 7 a) Teach, rebuke, correct, train us.
b) Personal.

THE WORD WORLDWIDE

We first heard of WORD WORLDWIDE over twenty years ago when Marie Dinnen, its founder, shared excitedly about the wonderful way ministry to one needy woman had exploded to touch many lives. It was great to see the Word of God being made central in the lives of thousands of men and women, then to witness the life-changing results of them applying the Word to their circumstances. Over the years the vision for WORD WORLDWIDE has not dimmed in the hearts of those who are involved in this ministry. God is still at work through His Word and in today's self-seeking society, the Word is even more relevant to those who desire true meaning and purpose in life. WORD WORLDWIDE is a ministry of WEC International, an interdenominational missionary society, whose sole purpose is to see Christ known, loved and worshipped by all, particularly those who have yet to hear of His wonderful name. This ministry is a vital part of our work and we warmly recommend the WORD WORLDWIDE 'Geared for Growth' Bible studies to you. We know that as you study His Word you will be enriched in your personal walk with Christ. It is our hope that as you are blessed through these studies, you will find opportunities to help others discover a personal relationship with Jesus. As a mission we would encourage you to work with us to make Christ known to the ends of the earth.

Stewart and Jean Moulds – British Directors, **WEC International**.

A full list of over 50 'Geared for Growth' studies can be obtained from:

John and Ann Edwards
5 Louvaine Terrace, Hetton-le-Hole, Tyne & Wear, DH5 9PP
Tel. 0191 5262803 Email: rhysjohn.edwards@virgin.net

Anne Jenkins
2 Windermere Road, Carnforth, Lancs., LA5 9AR
Tel. 01524 734797 Email: anne@jenkins.abelgratis.com

UK Website: www.gearedforgrowth.co.uk

Christian Focus Publications

publishes books for all ages

Our mission statement –

STAYING FAITHFUL

In dependence upon God we seek to help make His infallible word, the Bible, relevant. Our aim is to ensure that the Lord Jesus Christ is presented as the only hope to obtain forgiveness of sin, live a useful life and look forward to heaven with Him.

REACHING OUT

Christ's last command requires us to reach out to our world with His gospel. We seek to help fulfil that by publishing books that point people towards Jesus and help them develop a Christ-like maturity. We aim to equip all levels of readers for life, work, ministry and mission.

Books in our adult range are published in three imprints.

Christian Focus contains popular works including biographies, commentaries, basic doctrine, and Christian living. Our children's books are also published in this imprint.

Mentor focuses on books written at a level suitable for Bible College and seminary students, pastors, and other serious readers; the imprint includes commentaries, doctrinal studies, examination of current issues, and church history.

Christian Heritage contains classic writings from the past.

For details of our titles visit us on our website
www.christianfocus.com

Christian Focus Publications Ltd
Geanies House, Fearn, Tain,
Ross-shire, IV20 ITW, Scotland, United Kingdom.
info@christianfocus.com